Up in a Tree

Written by Catherine Baker
Illustrated by Neil Sutherland, Blue-Zoo and Tony Trimmer

The Alphablocks were hot.
"It will be cool under a tree," said T.

W... w... whoops! What is happening?

t-r-ee, tree!
All of a sudden, a tree began to appear ... right under w!

The tree got bigger ... and bigger!
W was stuck in the tree!
"Tut, tut!" said T. "Get down, W!"

"Oh no!" wept W. "I cannot get down!"
T had a plan.

b-l-a-n-k-e-t, blanket!
"What is that for?" said W. "It is far too hot for a blanket!"

"Jump down into the blanket," said T.
"Do not be afraid!"

But **W** **was** afraid.

"This tree is too high!" he said.

"I cannot jump!"

"This is no good," said T.
"We are still hot, and W is still stuck."

R and L were whispering.
Then they said, "We have a plan."
Their plan was good!

l-a-dd-er, ladder!
But the ladder was too short.
W was still stuck.

Just then, some Alphablocks went whizzing by.

"Stop!" said T. "Come and help us!"
P and H did come to help. They got ...

elephant

... an elephant!
The elephant stuck out its trunk, and
w slid right down it!

Terrific!

The elephant got **W** down ...
and the Alphablocks got a cool shower!